EARNEST SEEKERS OF TRUTH

by
Tyrell Nasheed Thabit

DEDICATION

This work is dedicated to my wife, Veronica, to my children, Angelica and Tyrell, my family, and all "Right-minded" people.

ACKNOWLEDGMENT

Firstly, I want to acknowledge the Creator of all the worlds, Allah (G_d), for this book would not be possible without His Mercy and Blessings. I am grateful to Imam Ronald B. Shaheed, for taking time from his busy schedule and lending his expertise, patience and time in helping me bring this project to fruition. To my son, Tyrell Jr., my gratitude and thanks are extended to you for your keen insight, proofreading skills and constructive criticism. You were very instrumental in assisting me in this endeavor. And last but not least, I want to acknowledge my wife, Veronica, for your continued support and understanding in allowing me to realize this dream.

Al-Fatiha (The Opening)

With G_d's Name, the Merciful Benefactor, the Merciful Redeemer.

Praise be to G_d, the Cherisher and Sustainer of the Worlds;

The Merciful Benefactor, the Merciful Redeemer

Master of the Day of Judgement.

Thee do we worship, And Thine aid we seek.

Show us the straight way,

The way of those on whom Thou hast bestowed Thy Grace.

Those whose (portion) is not wrath,

And who go not astray.

Holy Qur'an, Surah (Chapter) One, translation by Abdullah Yusuf Ali

Note: In order to show due reverence to the name of G_d Almighty, I have not used, in this publication, a spelling that can in the reverse spell, "dog".

Earnest Seekers of Truth
Published by Tyrell N. Thabit
Email: thabit.tyrell3@gmail.com

Grateful acknowledgment is made to G_d, the Almighty. He is One.

Printed in the United States of America.

Edited by Ronald B. Shaheed

Cover page by Zuhairah Shaheed

ISBN: 978-0-578-37529-8

Table of Contents

Author's Foreword

We don't know what's inside of us unless we look deep within and we will find that we're greater than we know. This will give us a higher knowledge and deeper insight into our life and where we should go with it. We have been empowered by our Lord, Sovereign and Creator, to elevate ourselves to great heights. We're blessed with the "power of thought", unlike the rest of creation, crowned, and given a colossal responsibility to guide mankind; to seek knowledge on every plane; whether it is in the deepest corner of the ocean, or the farthest planet in the universe.

We must harness this knowledge as a utility for the greater good of self and mankind, help and love one another the way G_d intended. This is the garden our Creator put us in, a body of knowledge, a condition we must cultivate with good works and our best intentions. To know G_d and His omnipotence and to know that He's Omnipresent, that is how we revere G_d, with His multifarious, innumerable Bounties and Blessings, which He Has bestowed on man in overflowing measure.

If G_d thinks enough of us to give us this kind of responsibility, shouldn't we think enough of Him to praise Him and strive to live according to His commandments? We put restraints and limitations on ourselves, never really knowing what our true essence is. G_d gave us five faculties, five points, like the star. He made us "all stars" and that should be our goal in life, to reach for our own star, by the Will of G_d.

Preface

Often times, we construe, or interpret diet to mean what we consume orally. That's true in one sense. In another, it literally means how we're living. It is based on what we internalize, or conceive in our soul and contain in our minds, things that allow negative concepts to mold and shape our attitudes and perceptions; holding on to things from the past; blaming others for where we are in our lives, and letting others dictate how we should live; also, thinking less of yourself when you know you are better than that.

It is important to our very being that we diligently apply ourselves in being mindful and staying away from environments that are contrary to our positive thinking. This publication, *"Earnest Seekers of Truth,"* is a plethora of subjects that deal with the diet of the soul. I touch on various subjects such as: "Every Tub Must Stand on Its Own Bottom; Message to Our Sister; Man Up, Our Own Holocaust and A House Divided", just to mention a few. I don't want to give all of them away. Just read my book. I think you'll enjoy it.

1

Every Tub Must Stand on Its Own Bottom

This is kind of a peculiar expression. It means we should learn to be accountable and responsible for our own actions and refrain from blaming others for where we are in our lives. We are all created equal with the ability and potential to excel in our own chosen field of endeavor. We are free to choose our own path in the pursuit of happiness and not give ourselves to the foolishness and temptations of this world.

That is what takes us off the path G_d designed for us. Did your Lord not create you and reveal to you the two highways (a choice between right and wrong)? The help of G_d is always near. Even when we're in the wrong, He's still working in and through us, bringing us back to the fold of righteousness. We must always hold on to the rope (your faith) that never breaks and we should never be afraid to defend each other, even when we're wrong. And how do we do this? "By holding your brother, or sister back from error" (a saying of Muhammed, the Prophet).

Charity Begins at Home

The upper hand is always better than the lower hand. Enough can never be said about the power of giving and that begins with self. Charity does begin at home (your internal home), and if you want to help others, establish and position yourself in a way where you can help your brother and sister. You can't rightly assist others if you are not in a good situation to do so. Who would loan to G_d a beautiful loan? When we come to the aid of our neighbor, G_d pays us back in ways beyond our understanding. His bounties are limitless. When G_d blesses us with material wealth, we should help each other. If enough of us follow this practice all over the world, we can wipe out poverty. Wouldn't you rather be paid by G_d than someone else? When you follow this way, G_d loves, favors you, and He informs the angels and they love you and pass the word throughout G_d's creation; and His creation loves you.

Jealousy

This word has been given a very negative connotation. Whenever it is used, the content is other than positive. Jealousy could, also, mean vigilant, or zealous, which means alertness, alive, sensitive, careful and conscious. Instead of being jealous and envious of one another, we should complement, applaud, and commend each other and be inspired by others' accomplishments and success. We should aspire to achieve and to have similar things. G_d said to worship Him, but don't forget to acquire some of this earth's richness. The earth is where all our material wealth comes from and we should want for our brother and sister what we want for ourselves. That is the meaning of a true believer.

Pride/Proud

I compound these two words because of their basic, fundamental meanings, which can be good, or bad. For instance, self-esteem, or self-respect, highly pleased, spirited, and glorious, these are all good when used in a positive way; for example, being proud of our children and their accomplishments, or taking pride in the things we do, and feeling good about them. These words can also have a negative connotation when used in an opposite way.

There are many negatives to these words, including but not limited to pride/proud; for example, haughty, arrogant, conceited, egotistic, snobbish and many more. These are the vices we must stay away from, because they can distract from our goodness and cause us to fall from G_d's Grace. Unfortunately, these iniquities have been the downfall for so many of us in our society. Being too proud, or prideful can cloud our judgment, or reasoning. This can get in the way and deter us from following the good in us. Humility is a very important element when interacting with others. Think about this the next time you're in a position that requires the best of yourself.

She Turned into a Pillar of Salt (Genesis 19:26)

What does this passage from the Bible (Old Testament) really mean? It means we need to stop looking behind and living in the past. If it was intended for us to look behind, our eyes would be placed in the back of our heads, instead of the front. They are in our forehead because we're supposed to look and think forward. Notice the direction our feet are pointed, in the frontal position. We're supposed to move forward in life, not backward. Salt is bitter, which means, if you're still talking about what someone did, or said to you years ago, you will become bitter. At the end of the day, the only thing we can really concentrate, or focus on is our present, because the future hasn't been created, yet. Treat your present as if it's your last day.

You should be about your business by prioritizing your schedule. Start a "Bucket list" of things you're going to do, today, and check them off as you accomplish them. If we orientate our day in this way, we will be surprised how much we can achieve and we will have a life full of happiness and bliss.

To Be or Not to Be

"I'm not going to be what you want me to be. I'm going to be what I want to be". This is a well-known quote by the late, great, Muhammad Ali, may G_d be pleased with him and grant him paradise. It's our inalienable right bestowed upon us by G_d to be whatever we want to be by His Will. We, sometimes, live our lives trying to please one another. There's nothing wrong with that, except we don't want to get caught up trying to pattern ourselves by other people's standards.

Instead, we should configure ourselves the way G_d wants us to be. G_d made us different so we may know one another and not be intolerant, controlling and despising each other. Any G_d-fearing person knows that G_d controls the universe and no matter what we think, we're not in charge of anything. Whatever befalls you was not going to pass you by, and whatever passes you by was not going to befall you. G_d made us different, and that includes our looks, smells, personalities, fingerprints, complexions, and more. If we were created alike, there wouldn't be any reason to talk to each other, to ask questions of each other, or to have any interaction, because we would all be the same. That is one of the reasons why we're made different. It keeps life interesting and it makes us attractive to each other.

2

"I've Have Been to the Mountain Top and Seen the Promised Land"

The above is a very well-known expression. Most of us think it was coined by the late, great, Dr. Martin Luther King, Jr. The truth is many people in history have said and ascended this station. Moses and Muhammed went to the mountain top and found the Promised Land (revelation). Harriet Tubman, Booker T. Washington, Frederick Douglas, Imam W. Deen Mohammed, El Hajj Malik Shabazz (Malcolm X), Marvin Gaye, Michael Jackson, Prince, President Barrack Obama, and a host of others have done the same.

We shouldn't look at this accomplishment from a physical standpoint. We should understand that, "Mountain top," and "Promised Land," can mean many things. In this instance, mountains, we know, are high up and things we accomplish in life are always on a higher level. So, the government in our lives should be of a higher consciousness. These are symbolic meanings, things we should elevate ourselves to.

Whether you are pursuing higher education, desiring to be in a better place with yourself, seeking promotion to a higher position on your job, or longing to be closer to the All-Knowing, the All-Merciful; whatever your endeavors and aspirations are they require advancement of your higher self. We all can get to the mountain top and see the Promised Land. Your only prerequisite is your unwavering faith in G_d, understanding of self, patience, perseverance; and soon your striving will be known.

Effect of Thought on Health and the Body

This is an excerpt from the book, *As a Man Thinketh*, by one of my favorite authors, James Allen. I highly recommend this book to the reader: "The body is the servant of the mind. It obeys the operations of the mind, whether they are deliberately chosen, or automatically expressed. At the bidding of unlawful thoughts, the body sinks rapidly into disease and decay; at the command of glad and beautiful thoughts' it becomes clothed with youthfulness and beauty".

He continues, "Disease and health, like circumstances, are rooted in thought. Sickly thoughts will express themselves through a sickly body. Thoughts of fear have been known to kill a person as effectively as a bullet. They are continually killing thousands of people just as surely, though less rapidly. The people who live in fear of disease are the people who get it. Anxiety quickly demoralizes the whole body and lays it open to the entrance of disease; while impure thoughts, even if not physically indulged, will soon shatter the nervous system. Strong, pure and happy thoughts build up the body with vigor and grace. The body is a delicate instrument, which responds readily to the thoughts by which it is impressed and habits of thought will produce their own effects upon it, good or bad. We will continue to have impure and poisoned blood, so long as we propagate unclean thoughts. Out of a clean heart comes a clean life and a clean body. Out of a defiled mind proceeds a defiled life and a corrupt body".

Allen, goes on to say, "Thought is the fount of action, life and manifestation; make the fountain pure and all will be pure. Change of diet will not help us if we're not willing to change our thoughts. When we make our thoughts pure, we no longer desire impure food. Clean thoughts, make clean habits. The so-called saint who does not wash his body is not a saint. He who has strengthened and purified his thoughts does not need to consider the malevolent microbe. If you would protect your body, guard your mind. If you would renew your body, beautify your mind. Thoughts of malice, envy, disappointment, despondency, rob the body of its health and grace. A sour face does not come by chance. It is made by sour thoughts. Wrinkles that mar are drawn by folly, passion and pride. I know a woman of age ninety-six who has the bright, innocent face of a girl. I know a man well under middle age whose face is drawn into inharmonious contours. The one is the result of a sweet and sunny disposition; the other is the outcome of passion and discontent, as you cannot have a sweet and wholesome abode unless you admit the air and sunshine freely into your rooms. "Therefore, a strong body and a bright, happy, or serene countenance can only result from the free admittance into the mind of thoughts of joy, goodwill and serenity. On the faces of the aged, there are wrinkles made by sympathy, others by strong and pure thoughts, and another we carve by passion. Who cannot distinguish them? With those who have lived righteously, age is calm, peaceful and softly mellowed, like the setting sun".

Finally, he says, "I have recently seen a philosopher on his deathbed. He was not old, except in years. He died as sweetly and peacefully as he had lived. There is no physician like cheerful thought for dissipating the ills of the body; there is no comforter to compare with goodwill for dispersing the shadows of grief and sorrow. To live continually in thoughts of ill will, cynicism, suspicion, and envy is to be confined in a self-made prison-hole. But to think well of all, to be cheerful with all, to patiently learn to find the good in all-such unselfish thoughts are the very portals of heaven; and to dwell day by day in thoughts of peace towards every creature will bring abounding peace to their possessor." (As A Man Thinketh, by James Allen; originally published in 1903)

Wealth and Happiness

It is interesting to look at the results of research on the relationship between one's wealth and happiness. Again, James Allen said: "Wealth is like health: Its utter absence can breed misery; yet, having it is no guarantee of happiness." Walter Dean Myers, renown author of young adult literature and recipient of many awards, presents the example of the United States. From 1957 to 1995, the after-tax income of the average citizen was more than doubled. But, although average Americans were richer, they were not one bit happier. In 1957, 35% said they were "Very happy", while 34% said the same in 2004.

The conclusion, regarding America, as well as, European countries, Australia, Japan and China, is that: "Economic growth in affluent countries has provided no apparent boost to morale, or social well-being." One could argue that people in these countries are more miserable, given the increase in crime, divorce, teen suicide and depression. Studies have, also, shown that people who strive the most to gain wealth tend to have low emotional well-being.

This is, especially, true for those who seek money to gain power, to show off, or to prove themselves. However, those who live with a sense of gratitude for what they have been blessed with, enjoy greater happiness. This is another example of research echoing what has already been confirmed by revelation. Gratitude should be directed to G_d, the Creator, the Source of all our provisions.

The Wisdom of the Spider and the Fly

A well-known, highly respected scholar, and my teacher, Imam W. Deen Mohammed, may G_d be pleased with him and grant him Paradise, gave this analogy in one of his public addresses, years ago. He had this to say on the subject and I am pleased to paraphrase it in here. He said a spider will build his web in the form of a circle. The fly will, inadvertently, find himself trapped in, or caught up, by the spider's web. Often times, this can be very destructive, or even fatal for the fly. If the fly stays in this condition too long it will diminish, becoming weak and frail, extracting all of its energy leaving nothing to build on. Over time, if you blow on what appears to be a fly while still in the spider's web, the only thing left, at this point, is dust.

This is a similitude to this world we live in. If we're not careful, we can find ourselves in this situation with no direction, or guidance; morally and physically weak from the bad influences and temptations of this world. In the book of Genesis (2:17), G_d is speaking to our earthly parents, (Adam and Eve), advising them to stay away from a particular tree in the garden.

This is a representation of the bad influences in this world. This

16

passage, also, goes on to mention the partaking of the apple. The apple can be a symbol of, or depict, ill intent; for instance, unhealthy foods that we eat every day. But we know that apples, like so many other fruits, are very healthy for us with properties that can guard against health issues. This is the path we want to take, by making better and well thought out decisions in our lives, if we want a better situation for ourselves and not end up like the fly.

Your Lord, Who created you said, "If you fear Him the way He wants you to, He will grant you a criterion to judge between right and wrong; remove from you all evil that may afflict you, and forgive you: For G_d is the Lord of grace unbounded". (Holy Qur'an, 3:74)

Man, in the Mirror

In the late 1980's, our dear brother, Michael Jackson, may G_d be pleased with him and grant him paradise, delivered a very important message to humanity. In one of his popular songs, he said he was going to, "Make a change, starting with the man in the mirror". He wasn't just referring to self. He stated, "We all need to make a change". When we look in the mirror, we see and feel the truth, internally and externally.

The problem for most of us is we're concerned only with the outside when the inside is much more important. Sometimes, it can be very difficult for some of us to accept the truth, especially, when it comes to self. Our heart/soul is the most significant component of our being. In Scripture, the heart is synonymous with the soul. We have to feed our soul with good works, i.e., be prayer-minded, read our Scripture every day, and treat others the way we want to be treated. When we go to sleep at night, the angels take our soul in order to record our deeds for that day. These actions are placed into a register. Afterwards, our soul is returned to us when we awake; if not, then we pass from this life.

G_d says all good comes from Him and all bad comes from that which we send forth with our own hands. What we call the ills of life are due to our own ill deeds. Every day, we all start out as venders of our own soul/heart, either freeing it, or bringing about its ruin. On the Day of Judgment, it will be said, "Read thy own record" (Holy Qur'an, 17:14). What most of us don't know is, we're in the judgment, now. This is the reason why some of us are in the condition, or a place, we're not too happy with. Don't wait until you pass through this life to do "Good works", because it could be too late. If we start with the, "Man/woman in the mirror", now, we can have a triple Paradise, in our heart/soul, in this life that we live in this objective world, and in the Hereafter, which is G_d's Eternal Home of Peace.

3

The Spirit of the Baby

One might ask what "The Spirit of the Baby" has to do with the subject of this book, or anything I've said so far? When a baby is born, its spirit is untainted. It hasn't been corrupted, or weakened by its environment. In spite of what some people may think, the baby is born without sin. The evidence is in the sweet fragrance of the baby. Have you ever noticed when the baby is born into this world, it has the sweet smell of musk? That's because the baby has been washed and perfumed by G_d.

When we are created our Creator gives us two angels that protect our right, left, front and back, recording any sins/infractions, or good deeds we may commit. When we commit an infraction, or sin, there's an "offensive odor" that emanates from our very being and is recorded as a violation on our soul. When we do good acts, or charities, a "sweet, agreeable aroma" is detected and registered as good deeds. At the time of the baby's advent, it only has one smell and that's the sweet one. Now, the baby is inaugurated into his/her chosen condition and almost immediately, the baby starts developing and growing to its full potential.

The baby starts out on his/her back, but the baby is not comfortable in this position. So, the baby, eventually, will change positions to his/her stomach. But, the baby isn't comfortable there, so, he/she gradually starts to pull up to a crawl position. Next, the baby is pulling up and walking along the walls of his/her surroundings. Once the baby builds up enough confidence he/she moves out on the faith G_d has instilled in the baby. The baby may fall down, sometimes, but he/she will get back up and start to walk and, eventually, the baby begins to run. That is because the baby's spirit is uninhibited. We, as adults and believers in G_d, have to revert back to the "Spirit of the baby". The different levels I've given you above of the baby can, also, be viewed, symbolically, as vicissitudes, or our ups and downs in life. At some point in our lives as grownups, we've all been in these different positions.

We're going to have them, because G_d has made us to toil and struggle in this world as a test of our faith in Him. Do you think you're going to be left alone on merely saying, "I believe"? G_d does not accept lip service, only the pure intentions in our soul. That is the reason why there are calamities that sometime come into our lives as a test from G_d. Once this happens and we pass the test, G_d blesses us with greater prosperity. When we travel back through the annals of time, we find that all Messengers, Prophets, Sages, Saints, and G_d-fearing people throughout history were tested with life's challenges. They passed their test and were blessed with spiritual and earthly riches. And if it is G_d's Will, we will all earn the Paradise.

A Message to Our Sisters

Since the dawn of time, the woman has always been an invaluable entity to the man. Today, she is just as important as she ever was and always will be. Before woman was created, man was incomplete. He was without a companion; the angels didn't have time for him because they were too busy worshiping their Lord and Satan would ridicule and make fun of man. One day the angels visited man and noticed there was a new form of creation in his presence. They inquired about this strange phenomenon and man told them that she was a woman, his companion/wife, not his girlfriend. She was laying above his head comforting him.

Notice when you (men) and your spouse are in bed, or on the couch, she's rubbing your head and you're exchanging sweet pleasantries. This is one of the most comforting positions to be in with your mate. Have you ever had a tough day at work and couldn't wait to come home to her? Her smile, alone, is so soothing to you; so much so, until when you walk through the door and you see that person who can enrich your life on so many levels, your fears, disappointments, and insecurities disappear. If you tell her about your day, she knows just what to say to make you feel better. This clearly demonstrates the importance of having her as your wife and companion.

This is the picture we should get from this message. This is exactly what our society is missing, the solace and consolation of the woman G_d made. He has given Heaven to man through her. She is the man's society and he couldn't exist without her. Prophet Muhammed said, "Paradise is at the feet of the woman". Her feet represent her support and contribution to this world we live in. Genesis (2:22), talks about the woman being made from the rib of the man. The rib it's talking about is the one closest to the heart. The heart represents our emotions, feelings, and passions. This, also, represents the Church, which can play on our sentiments. This particular rib is curved and if you try to straighten it, you will break it. This is her spirit and before she allows you to do this, she will leave you.

Down through history, it is unfortunate that our sisters have been despised, overlooked, disregarded, passed over, ignored, and neglected. It stands to reason that she may now be bitter, scornful, acrimonious, hard, disgruntled, cold and discontented. In some cases, she has lost her way and without her, we will never ascend to a level of fulfillment and have heaven here on earth, as men. Some men have gone so far as to say that the woman is evil. Scripture came to correct all of this and elevate the woman to her rightful status. If you look into our society, you will see that the woman is favored in every arena.

From the chess board, to the clothing store, the courtroom, public assistance, employment, women are favored. If you see a man mistreating her in your presence, if you're a real man you will discourage this kind of behavior. G_d will surely punish you, if you disrespect her. Brothers, your woman will never give you the map to her heart until you give her the respect she deserves. If you want her heart, you have to go where few men have gone and that is allowing her to completely trust you. Sisters, elevate your standards. Expect more of yourself. This means, by the way you dress, speak, look, and carry yourself. If you do this, you will raise the yardstick when it comes to the men G_d chooses for you in your life.

Sisters, you have always been in the driver's seat. You are in command. Have you ever heard the expression, "Behind every good man is a good woman"? Some women may misunderstand this statement, because they're standing behind their man, and that seems to put them in an inferior position. This can't be further from the truth. This is not to be taken, literally. Sometimes, we as men, can become complacent, lazy, or too comfortable in our present situation. Sometimes, we need to be motivated and encouraged by our mate in order to keep going. Things can be very hard on us, as men, if we don't have the love and support of our partner. The trouble is a lot of our women have lowered the banner of their own excellence when it comes to self. The real men of this world want you to come back to the community of your true nature. After all, we can't afford to lose the only true comforter and friend made especially for us here on earth, by the One Who is Wise and All-Knowing.

Man Up!

Do you know what a vicegerent is? It's what G_d called man (the human being) when he put him here on earth. He's a General, a Leader, G_d's representative. One day, G_d had a conversation with the Angels, telling them He was going to make His man; and when He finished, the Angels would have to pay their respect, along with the Jinn. The Angels followed G_d's command, but not the Jinn, who said that He was better, because He was made from fire and man was made from mud. This story of how the Jinn became the Satan is outlined in Chapter 2 of the Holy Qur'an.

The story goes on to say that because of his attitude and disposition, the Jinn took on another form, called Iblis, one who rebelled against G_d's Will. He believed that man wasn't good enough for Him to admire, or respect. Eventually, Iblis decided that he had to prove he was better than the man G_d was making and vowed to do things to prove man's inferiority, if given time;

thus, Satan, the enemy of man, was manifested. This is evidence of Satan's narrow-mindedness. What Satan did not know was mud is made from dirt and water, which can smother fire and put it out. Furthermore, Satan failed to realize who was giving him the command to acknowledge this new creation. Satan, also, said he would come after man from all sides. G_d said, "If you do, I will fill hell with you all". So, G_d granted Satan's respite.

Man, you are living in pure Hell. You have failed to realize and cherish the wombs that bore you. (Holy Qur'an 4:1). Brothers, you can amass all the materialism in this world, but you will never be right with G_d, until you start treating your woman with the reverence she deserves. In the Book of Genesis (3:6), it says the woman bit of the "Forbidden fruit," and afterwards, she influenced man to do the same. This paints a very negative picture of the woman, because this Scripture has been misread, according to Imam W. Deen Mohammed, who said woman, in Scripture is talking about community, or society. In commenting on this, Imam Mohammed said:

"The Qur'an says that the devil deceived Adam and his wife, which means the original forms and dispositions in the intellect. The intelligent nature, that is Adam, and the perception of the environment that must feed that intelligent nature so that it grows and becomes more and more efficient in a real environment, in a real natural world, that is Eve. What you feed is Eve. You have to feed it, that which you have from the outer, external world. The Satan caught on to that and he deceived Adam out of his nature. The Bible gives the picture that Satan gave it to the woman and she fed it to the man. But the Qur'an corrects

24

that and says, "No, he gave it to both of them". It did not reach the man from the woman. Satan reached both the man and the woman. He deceived both the intelligent nature and the perception. The ability to perceive the world and reality, that is the woman. She is the concept and in her we are formed. So, really, the mother, our physical, or biological mother, in Scripture, is the first environment and it is to point us to another birth in the external environment, just like we are put into our mother as a germ to develop and mature into a complete physical form of a human being and then she delivers us. We are delivered from her body, which means from that world (Imam W. Deen Mohammed, *The Women Who Call to the Issue*, p. 6, 2018).

I have read further, in history, that if a woman had a girl, it was frowned upon. If we think about this long and hard, why would G_d disfavor the one who He used as a vessel to bring about His human creation? That's one of G_d's many great mercies that is not to be taken lightly. Brothers, you treat your woman like you really believe she's bad; not just in America, but in most parts around the globe. The more you mistreat her the more hell will come into your life. You have gone so far as to put a dog in front of her as your best friend. You will never soar and have the kind of bounties G_d has in store for you, if you continue this senseless abuse of the woman He made especially for you.

One of the ways man will earn the Paradise is through his fair and just treatment to his woman. That's by supporting and helping her progress to the level where G_d wants her to be. You're her helpmeet/helpmate and she's yours. When we look out into creation, we see government, order, beauty and structure. We as men, need to put these entities back into our lives. If you're not where you need to be, physically, emotionally, intellectually, educationally, spiritually, materially, and financially, don't bring your sister down with you. Don't fecundate her, if she's not your wife and you're not ready to bring a life into this world.

If you love her, give her your last name, first, so she can feel proud and not be confounded with shame and embarrassment. If she has your baby and not your name your future together will definitely be uncertain. Don't move her into a house, or an apartment as your girlfriend, or fiancé. G_d didn't authorize shacking. You did, because you're being influenced by Satan. If your wife does not want to work, she shouldn't have to and we, as men, should provide for her on a very generous level. If she wants to work, it should be her choice and her right. She earned it. You're wondering why everywhere you turn hell is in your life. Satan told you He will come after you from all sides, and if you follow his way (Satan), G_d said He will fill both of your lives with damnation, if you disobey Him. Men, we are protectors and maintainers of our sisters. The Creator of the Heavens and the Earth says: "Man Up!"

What's Going On?

Many of us want to know, "What's Going On?" This is an expression derived from a song from the late, great, rhythm and blues artist, Marvin Gaye, may G_d bless him and grant him paradise. To this day, the expression still rings true. "What's Going On", in our world, today? Before man was ever thought of, there was a time when G_d was having a conversation with the Angel, Jibril, or the Angel, Gabriel.

G_d was showing the Angel, Jibril, through a monitor, or a screen, this world we live in before Satan influenced it. There were no wars, famine, diseases, unemployment, senseless killings, deaths, unwanted pregnancies, premarital sex, promiscuous sex, illegal drugs, man-made religions, crack, depression, premature aging due to stress and worry, and alcoholism. The list goes on and on. When the Jibril saw this, He said, "With a world like this, how can man go wrong?" Then G_d showed Jibril, a preview of the world after Satan put his influence on it. Everything mentioned above was in complete opposition. After seeing this, the Angel said, "With a world like this, how can man go right?"

This was G_d's providence to man, that He promised him Gardens beneath which rivers flow, if he followed G_d's command. G_d never breaks His Covenant. It wasn't G_d who strayed from His Will, or His Word, because G_d is unchanging. It was man. Surely, we can't innovate, or change G_d's dictates and live the way we want to and expect to earn His favors.

Man, the human being, was given a will and choices. This was only a test from G_d, the same way Prophet Abraham and His son Prophet Ishmael, Peace be upon them, were tested. This wasn't to put man in a better situation than the rest of G_d's creation, because the only real choice for man is to follow G_d's Will, if he wants earthly satisfaction and an even better happenstance in the next life. This world man has created for himself is the result of his wayward desires and his own undoing. The only way man can fix the problems he created is to come back to the Lord and Cherisher of all Worlds. We only worship G_d when it is convenient for us. We have to make Him our first priority, not just when we want to, or when we're in trouble, or want something.

If you forget G_d, He will forget you on the Day of Judgment. Imam W. Deen Mohammed, in one of his many scholarly public addresses said, "We're in the Day of Religion". If Marvin Gaye were to come back today, I believe he would still ask the question, "What's Going On?"

Rediscovery of Self

I have talked about a myriad of things, thus far. Now, I want to talk about one of the most important things we can do for ourselves. We do many things for our outer self, but how much do we do for our internal being? My dear sisters and brothers, our lives must now begin. Rediscovery is about reaching down deep and mining out who we really are. G_d said He made us all great, with unlimited potential, and gave us all many job descriptions. It's up to you and I to find out what they are and your Lord will help you.

We must stop prohibiting ourselves from realizing our true greatness G_d has blessed us with through our innate abilities. We have to stop being afraid to try because of the fear of failure. We have to understand that there is no success without failure. All successful people have one thing in common. They all failed more than once before becoming successful. We have to come out of our cocoon of comfort and complacency to explore rediscovery of self.

The only limits we have are the ones we put on ourselves. We will never prosper at anything if we don't push ourselves. Stop being satisfied with the status quo. We're part of G_d's great creation and vast universe, which literally has no limitations and neither do we.

Don't Know Where You're Going

This is a problem that has been plaguing African Americans since the days of slavery. It is the hate for self and division among each other, introduced to us by the slave master, that is still going on today. There was a time in our history when we had self-love in everything we did. The killing of our sisters and brothers in this country, today, has reached an alarming rate.

Many of us are still plagued with these debaucheries. That's only because we don't know our history. Once we study and learn who we truly are and the great calamities our forefathers and mothers had to bear, the more appreciation and love we will have for ourselves and each other. There have been many "great ones" who came before us, that lived, suffered, and died so that we may have restored dignity and self-love.

If some of these warriors/vanguards who died on the battlefields of America, came back, they would rebuke the senseless killings, drug abuse, and immorality that is going on, every day, in our communities. We must kick these slave habits and the inferior thinking that we have inflicted ourselves with in ways no other people have seen in the history of this country. Down through the ages, time has shown overwhelming evidence that we are a people of great fortitude. It is said that, "If you don't know your story and where you've been, you sure as hell don't know where you're going".

Your sisters and brothers are not your enemy. You are taking out your aggression on them because of your own self-hatred. "If black lives matter", why not start with a "cease fire" against ourselves and each other. Bring an end to this civil war that's been going on between us since we were brought here, shackled in chains. My dear ones, we're standing on the "Edge of the world." We're our own weapons of mass destruction. If we don't save ourselves, one day, we could become extinct.

4

The "N" Word

The following is an excerpt from the *African American Registry*: "The "N" Word. It is one of the most notorious words in American culture. Some words carry more weight than others. Without trying to exaggerate, is genocide just another word? Clearly, no, and neither is the, "N" Word. After a period of relative dormancy, the "N" Word, has been reborn in popular culture. It is hard-edged, streetwise, and it has crossed over into movies, like *Pulp Fiction* (1994) and *Jackie Brown* (1997), where it became a symbol of "street authenticity" and hipness.

"Denzel Washington's character in the movie, *Training Day* (2001), uses the, "N" Word, frequently and harshly. Richard Pryor, long ago, rejected the use of the word in his comedy act. But Chris Rock, Chris Tucker, and other Black male, comedy kings, use the "N" Word, regularly, and not affectionately. Justin Driver, a social critic, makes a case that both Rock and Tucker are modern minstrels, shucking, jiving, and grinning, in the tradition of comedic actor, Stepin Fetchit. White supremacists have found the internet as an indispensable tool for spreading their message of hate."

"An Internet search of the, "N" Word, using Netscape, or Alta Vista, locates many anti-Black web pages: 'Niggers Must Die'; 'Hang a Nigger for America'; 'Nigger Joke Central', and many others. Web searchers find what most Blacks know from personal experience, that the, "N" Word, is an expression of anti-black hostility. Without question, the "N" Word, is the most commonly used racist slur used during hate crimes. There is so much to be said about probably the most offensive word in the English dictionary."

"James Baldwin said: 'You can only be destroyed by believing that you really are what the white world calls a nigger.' For those of you who are not sure of the definition of this repugnant word, we strongly encourage you to study and closely examine its meaning. Maybe then you will think twice about its utility in your expressions" (*The African American Registry*, a comprehensive on-line database resource of African American heritage).

Relationships

Many may differ with the following comments on the subject of relationships. If we look closely at the ramifications, consequences, and pitfalls of being involved in this kind of union, you will find that the chances of emerging with your feelings still intact are very slim. Oftentimes, the aftermath leaves us discombobulated and emotionally scarred from the lying, misuse, abuse, fornicating, arguing, commitment issues, cheating, and if children are involved, you have to deal with each other until they are at least 18 years of age and, sometimes, beyond. This is the cause of enmity and hatred between you and your former partner.

If we peruse every Scripture, every holy book, never will we find where G_d has sanctioned premarital sex relationships. When G_d created man and woman, they were not boyfriend and girlfriend. They were husband and wife. We, as human beings, cannot trespass the parameters G_d has commissioned for us. We catch so much hell as a result of trying to go against what G_d has preordained for mankind.

G_d wants us to follow the right path. When we choose our own way of thinking, though we know what's right, we often end up in a predicament where we're sorry and have regrets. There are no standards in premarital relationships. We do whatever we want. When G_d gave us to each other, along with that, He gave us a standard. If you can afford it, marry and treat and honor each other with respect and G_d will bless your matrimony with countless bliss.

Brothers and sisters, we don't have to live upside down, when we can live right side up. There are countless dating sites, books, and counselors who want to be experts on relationships. They think they can demean what G_d has setup. Clearly, we have become an arrogant and pompous people, thinking we know what's best for the human being; when it was G_d who Willed the creation of the human family. We were merely used as vessels. It was G_d who made the deposit and brought about humanity. Wouldn't you rather have the kind of happiness G_d wants for you instead of whatever?

Still at the Back of the Bus

We have been very successful in every arena in this country, in sports, Fortune 500 companies, medicine, law, politics, and now, the presidency of these United States (i.e., President Barack Obama). In spite of the great strives we have made as a people, we are still sitting and standing around waiting to be told what to do and how to do it. G_d said He made us in the best mold and gave us the ability to pursue knowledge in every facet of His creation.

Rosa Parks, may G_d be pleased with her and grant her paradise, her soul wouldn't allow her to be content and satisfied with the conditions of this country and the African American plight in her day. Her courageous act infused a significant part of the civil rights movement. She stood up to be heard and to take her place in history among the greats. That's exactly what she wanted for you and I. Rosa Parks gave us a picture of what we should be as men and women. She wanted us to stand up for ourselves and come forward. We, as a people, are still at the "back of the bus" of our lives, in our present condition.

We must promote ourselves in a way that will earn us self-respect, through competing in the job market, being good, law-abiding citizens, and protecting and enjoying the rights our forefathers and mothers fought and died for. We're spending too much of our precious time playing games on our cell phones, with social media, running to the tattoo parlor, and listening to corrupt music. We must not allow ourselves to be preoccupied with trivial and unimportant matters. We live in a vast universe with enough riches for all.

This is G_d's paradise He gave to His human creation to cherish and enjoy. We are not created to sit around being afraid, worrying and complaining about what we don't have. When you talk about the world being a messed-up place, that's your world. G_d said He is sufficient for the believer, and will provide whatever we need. Take it to G_d and He will tell you to look within yourselves and you will find the answer to all of your problems; because in you, you will find G_d. He resides in all of His creation.

We should stop relying so much upon human beings because they can, sometimes, let you down. If G_d gives you something, it was intended for you to have and you should praise Him. If He takes something away from you, it's only as a test and He will bless you with something greater. If G_d didn't give you what you asked for, you should still praise Him, because it may not be time for you to have it right now; and G_d is the best knower of all and He's always on time. Therefore, whatever we strive for in this life, strive in the name of your Merciful Creator.

Frankenstein

One might ask, what is a Frankenstein? It's an experiment gone bad. Over the course of time, people with ill intent have taken words from Scripture to serve their own purpose. For instance, in the Bible, it says, *"Let us make man in our image and after our likeness"*. (Genesis 1:26). These words were taken out of context and used to enslave a people in a way that would make them subservient to another people; so, they would rule over them for an indefinite period of time.

This attempt failed. The people enslaved in this country, with the help of others, started a revolt and rose up against their rulers. More and more, the rulers started losing control over the servants, which is why you had the birth of the Underground Railroad, Nat Turner, and other defiant persons and groups. After this hideous experience, conditions, gradually, got better for a people who the slave master thought were inferior to him.

Do you remember the old Frankenstein movies? After a failed experiment went wrong, the only choice left was to put an end to the monster; because in the master's mind, this Frankenstein got out of control. There was fear that he would do a great deal of harm, or take over; which brings us to the killing of young, African American males, today. This experiment is being fueled by drugs, guns, welfare, bad living conditions, weak concepts, high unemployment rate, and many other social ills in the black community. It was thought that this would keep the African American docile, lethargic and content.

The "Powers that Be" knew when our forefathers and mothers were brought here, chained and bound, in the bellies of ships against their will and were made to do things our ancestors knew in their souls was wrong, that this would, later on, bring trouble; and lead to uprisings and protests. Our young men are being shot down in the streets across the U. S. because they're part of this same experiment to eradicate the black race. This is why the killings and unjustified imprisonment of our young men are just another day at the office for the police department and the so-called legal system. There is a book in circulation called: *"Breaking Rank"*, by Norm Stamper. This great work is a top cop's expose of the dark side of American policing. If we want this type of policing to stop, we need laws in America that will legislate change, to hold these few police officers to strict accountability; and heavy penalties should be paid for this kind of brutality. A policeman/policewoman's job is to serve and protect the citizens of this country and not to kill us, black people, in particular.

It is written that there will come a day when men will be so scarce, a woman will be seen carrying a bone of a dead man and she will be asked: "Why are you carrying that bone of a dead man?" And she will say, "This is the bone of a good man!" That time has come, my dear sisters. It is hard to find, "a good man". Our black men are being systematically dehumanized through the worse system of abuse imaginable.

Dumb Dogs Cannot Bark

The Bible, in the book of Isaiah (56:10), speaks to this expression. It is talking about a mindset of a people. When we observe the bark of a tree, it means a mentality that can see no deeper than what is on the surface. So, they are "dumb dogs". They cannot bark. This is the orientation for most of us in our learning. It's unfortunate that we haven't rid our minds of this yoke that has burdened us far too long. Even in some of our houses of worship, we only get the surface of the message and that's the words off the pages.

We seem to fall short of what's really being conveyed. If we want to be guided in this world, it can only be done by the correct understanding and wisdom of what our Scriptures are giving us. We must go behind the words and penetrate what's really being said. It doesn't stop there. We must learn to read G_d's creation, which, also, has an opulent meaning. You can teach a parrot to mimic words, but he doesn't know what he's saying. G_d created us to reason, ponder and reflect.

If we're not doing this, then we're no different than the aforementioned bird. Knowledge without wisdom is like a tree without roots. Knowledge must marry wisdom, and wisdom has to support knowledge, if we want our understanding to be complete. Remember, there's always a richer and higher meaning beneath the surface of all things. An author by the name of Professor Arnold Ehret said, "The main trouble with the average individuals of present-day civilization is that they refuse to think".

Whether you're reading a book, watching television, or pondering on G_d's great creation, there will always be a hidden, or deeper meaning. We have to be, like miners. We have to dig out these jewels. We must unlock them with the keys of understanding that are in each and every one of us.

Saggin/Niggas

With all the trends that have graced the fashion stage, this one has to be, by far, the worse. With every style there's always a message underneath. Judge Mathis wrote an article, some years ago, explaining this, "Repugnant look", that originated on the prison yards of America. It means you're inviting anyone who's interested, to your posterior (i.e., ass). Over a period of time, there have been written documents/correspondence on people of color with the intent to view them as uncivilized, giving them an inferior image, or targeting the underbelly of their culture. This can only be accomplished when we supply the ammunition that is needed through our poor, immature behavior. Wherever a trend starts, it always settles, or ends in the black community. Our culture will continue to be a landfill as long as we continue to project ourselves as a people with no sense of independence, direction, or free thinking; relying on the media and the government to tell us what to think, where to live; how to dress, what to eat; what to say, and how to carry ourselves; as if we're being seen as livestock. Every human being wants to be treated with respect. This will never happen if we persist in allowing ourselves to be a sheepish people.

5

The Addams Family

Whenever Hollywood wants to make a movie, or a television show, they look into our society to find something dysfunctional to use; and then they capitalize on the vulnerable areas of the American culture as a premise for their storyline. Consequently, what we see on the silver screens and on television screens are reflections of what is going on in the American family, and our society. There was a television show that aired in the 1970's called, "*The Addams Family*". Everyone in that family had a peculiar, or weird disposition; a commentary on the status of American families in the 1970's.

This still applies, today, among many of us who have issues such as, drug addiction, loneliness, depression, paranoia, or some other abnormal behavior. That is because the American family is losing its way. We're gradually getting away from the things that matter, like G_d and family. No matter how we choose to differentiate between each other, the human family is one, and G_d is One. As individuals, our differences and our distinctiveness are our strengths, not our weakness. We see ourselves as a nation of many races. However, the only true race is the human race. We can't allow ourselves to get away from this reality and become a nation of tribes.

We are haters of one another because of the way we were, systematically, orientated because of slavery, the Civil War, etc. We were created from one being, and our human father's name is

Adam. This is the "Adams Family" G_d wants us to be a part of. G_d wants us to be in a race, inviting to all that is good; not the biased one the media invites us to embrace through the promulgation of its capricious and freaky ideas that they perceive to be normal.

Learning Begins at Home

If you're like most people, you're probably thinking about the home you're sitting in, right now. Well, you can't be further from the truth. The home I'm talking about is the mother's womb. A child's nurturing starts there. It's very important that we understand, when a woman and a man decide to have children, the first requirement is marriage. Secondly, it should be a planned pregnancy. The third is not being under the influence of alcohol, or drugs. This can definitely affect the child's mental and physical wellbeing.

Did you know, prior to laying down and having sexual congress with your "spouse," you should say a prayer, asking G_d to bless this very special and close intimacy. Otherwise, you will involve Satan as a third party and this is how his (Satan's) offspring are born. G_d said He made us in the best mold (Holy Qur'an 95:4). When G_d gives us children, with that, He gives us maternal and paternal instincts as a guide to show us how we should be as parents. We change that by going against G_d's blueprint by putting our children in an environment that is non-conducive to the baby's natural growth, since the baby's time of birth.

Bad children come from bad intentions and actions of the parents. During a woman's gestation time, she should read Scripture to her baby and she should pray, as much as she can, for a strong, healthy child. She should not experience excessive stress, or ponder over negative thoughts. She should be conscious of her diet and her supplements. Once the child is ushered into this life, it is of paramount importance that the child be breast fed, because of the antibiotics and goodness in the mother's breast milk. This will allow for the baby proper development, and a chance to grow up healthy, both physically and mentally, and to have significantly fewer sick days and health issues.

Once the baby is taken off breast milk, a well-balanced diet should continue. This means little, or no fast foods, or foods with no nutritional value. Studies show this can affect a child's learning and behavior for the rest of their life; also, a child's learning should not end after school. Our learning starts in the cradle, and should end only in the grave. We should always cherish and respect our parents, if we want peace in our lives. *"Honor thy father and thy mother, that thy days may be long"* (Exodus 20:12). *"And We have enjoined on man (to be good) to his parents"*. (Holy Qur'an 31:14). We should always seek to remain in a positive environment and that's by asking G_d to bless us with healthy thoughts and to help us to put the best construction on everything we do. Our Lord gives special bounties to the ones who are careful of their duties to Him, at all times. *"Those who reject G_d, will assuredly never prosper"*. (Holy Qur'an 28: 82).

Parents should introduce their children to the institution of prayer and they must understand we can't exist properly without G_d's help. Parents (for those of you who are not aware of this) should never beat, or yell at their children. For Black people, this is a carryover from slavery. It will only make them rebel and it may

42

cause them to have a nervous condition. Talk to them. This will lead to strong communication and a wonderful understanding. These are two of the greatest things to have with your children.

A Message of Concern by Imam W. Deen Mohammed

The following is a passage from a book called, *Noah's Flood*, by my teacher, Imam W. Deen Mohammed, and it gives me great pleasure to bring this excerpt to you:

"A doctor once was hearing the complaints of his patient and his patient didn't really have any real complaints, except in his mind. The complaints were of the mind, not of the physical body, and this person was living a very unhappy life and needed too much help; needed more help than some two-year-old children expect. So, the doctor had been struggling with this patient for a long time, and the doctor said, 'I'm going to give you a different prescription, today'; and the patient said, 'What is it?' 'Forget about yourself and go out and find somebody that needs some help and help them.' And, sometimes, that's the only way you can get help for your own self. You have to take your mind off of your own problems, and off of your own self, and find somebody as miserable as you are, or more miserable; and go try to help them and that will be the cure for you."

G_d Who So Loved the World Gave His Only Begotten Son to Atone for Our Sins.

This misinterpreted and misunderstood concept has caused extremely damaging circumstances to humanity; especially to the ones who are devoid of understanding; people who feel they can

43

do anything they want, without any consequences. As a consequence, not being accountable, or responsible for their actions makes them very immature individuals. G_d wants us to grow and develop into mature believers. When we travel back through time, we find that the world has always been a world of sin.

This is the reason for the sending of thousands of Messengers, Prophets, saints, sages, and wise men, in order to bring mankind back to righteousness. The world fed us this concept, that G_d sacrificed His so-called son, Christ Jesus, for our sins and we continue to sin to this day. A lot of good that did! If G_d is Good, why would He advocate evil in the world? In Romans (12:19), it says, *"Vengeance is mine; I will repay, said the Lord"*. Clearly, G_d hates evil. Why would He sacrifice Christ Jesus for the wickedness of the world? We need to stop being a culture of fishes, opening our mouths and closing our minds, allowing ourselves to be hooked by anything.

6

The Lord of All the Worlds

G_d created the Heavens and earth, life and death. Scientists tell us that seventy-eight percent of the earth is populated with water and the earth is only twenty-two percent mass. Mathematically, that is an imbalance. Who do you think is holding back the water? If G_d can manage this and everything in the universe 24/7, surely, He can save our souls. Having faith in G_d means to believe with certainty and conviction that G_d is the Lord and Sovereign of all that exists. He is the Creator, Planner, and Sustainer of the entire universe. G_d is One, without partners, and deserves to be worshipped as the One G_d. He has the most exalted and perfect attributes. He is far above having any faults, or defects.

Good Friday

We're told that Christ Jesus died on a Friday and came back three days later. If you add the days up, that will give you Monday. Mathematically, two days, later will give you so-called, Easter Sunday. Now we're worshiping a rabbit. The rabbit is symbolically representing pornography. We know that Easter is celebrated on a different date every year between March 22 - April 25. This is established by a complex set of calculations, based on observations of the moon, meaning the date is different every year. Now, the Friday before so-called Easter Sunday is, supposedly, when Christ Jesus passed away, or was killed on a cross. If this is the case, that means Christ Jesus has a different death date every year. Including Christ Jesus, no human being has ever died in this life and physically came back in the same life. G_d does not permit that we experience death and come back and tell the living. This is a lower life for us, and as believers in G_d, we should believe there's a better and higher life. Including Christ Jesus, why would anyone want to die and come back to a world full of transgressions, debt, trouble, disappointment, and chronic problems, none of which, are in the hereafter? That's the life we should all want to be a part of. Moreover, G_d has promised, whoever enters the heavenly paradise would never leave it. In other words, there is no exit door. (Holy Qur'an 15:48).

We Are Not Deities

Many times, we place too much emphasis on each other, thinking that we can address all of our needs. We fail every time, trying to hold each other to a standard we're not willing to hold ourselves to; thinking way too high of one another, when we, as human beings, will always have imperfections. There has never been a perfect human being on this earth. If we're expecting perfection in each other and the world we live in, then what can we expect in the next life? That's the reason why it makes no sense to come back to this life once you pass through. The next life is perfect.

Feet the Color of Brass, Eyes Red and Hair Like Wool

Let us apply our deductive reasoning, here, for just a moment. Have you ever seen someone in your life who looks like the picture given of Jesus Christ in the Scripture? The so-called representation of Christ Jesus, given in the Bible, sounds like a bum. When we look around in our houses of worship, we see a man of light complexion. I'm convinced that in order to follow a concept like this, you would have to abandon your sanity, because you can't have two different physical descriptions. The problem with the world is we want to worship man as a deity, or bring G_d down to a human, or physical form. What difference does it make what color Christ Jesus was? What matters, is his message, the one he was inspired with and received from the One Who Knows the mysteries of the Heavens and Earth.

Christmas Day

It is believed, by Christians, that 2,000 years ago Christ Jesus was born in Israel to his mother, Mary. Now, I know one might think, who was his father? If we study the creation of humanity, there were three different ways mankind was conceived: Between man and woman, without a man, nor a woman (Adam and Eve), and Christ Jesus, to his mother Mary, of virgin birth. This is not a stretch for G_d. All He has to say is, "Be, or Behold!" and it is just like He created everything else, from nothing but a word.

When Mary experienced the pains of childbirth, like any other woman, revelation from G_d came to her saying: *"Grieve not! For thy Lord Hath provided a rivulet (a small stream) beneath thee; And shake towards thyself the trunk of the palm tree; It will let fall fresh ripe dates upon thee. So, eat and drink and cool (thine) eye".* (Holy Qur'an 19:24-26). Mary washed up after her delivery, because there were no doctors around and she ate dates and drank water. If you know anything about dates, you will know, like any other fruit, they only grow during the warm months and not December 25; besides, Christmas was never celebrated in Israel.

7

The So-called Crucifixion of Christ Jesus

If you look up the word, "Crucifixion", you will find that it means, "To mortify, torture, and persecute", among other things. The so-called crucifixion of Christ Jesus, has a deep and symbolic meaning. Let's start with the historical picture of a man on a so-called cross, or a stick. Notice the thorny crown on his head. It is showing you that he's being enslaved through mental bondage. He's being oppressed by mind control. His hands and feet are nailed to a stick and he looks depressed and humiliated.

The so-called cross that Christ Jesus was supposedly tied to is really a sword, if you look at it up-side down. Sword represents death, or the killing of a people, or even a race of people. It was also said, while Jesus was on this so-called cross, He asked G_d why did He forsake him. Forsaken, means, "to abandon, desert, to leave". If you know anything about your history, you would know that we were stolen from Africa, and sold into slavery. So, the rulers, or the government of that day, had to have had a hand in this inhumane crime against our people; because you can't visit a continent and steal that many denizens over a long period of time without the knowledge, assistance, or cooperation from the local, or state governments.

So, you see, G_d didn't forsake Jesus. It was our African ancestors who left us desolate. Isn't this a similitude of our treatment in America? We have suffered more in this country and have been subjected to the most repugnant treatment of any people on record. We continue to allow ourselves to be treated this way, in the name of Christ Jesus, because we think it will bring us closer to him and make us Christ-like. Some years ago, I was watching a movie about Christ Jesus and in the movie, he had to bear, or carry a so-called cross on his back. This is a symbol, or symbolic picture showing us as human beings, we have to bear our own cross in this life.

The Real Crucifixion

Christ Jesus never died on a cross. Why would G_d allow this to happen to one of His most eminent Messengers? He wouldn't give Christ Jesus revelation, then allow him to be killed by the wicked. That doesn't make any sense; besides, that would make G_d look weak and powerless. It would make G_d look like He didn't have Christ Jesus' back. So, the next time you see someone with a so-called cross around their neck, representing the so-called crucifixion of Christ Jesus, in reality, it's perpetuating our treatment in this country; since our forefathers and mothers were dragged here, with no suitcase, in the belly of slave ships and treated so badly until many of them committed suicide.

If we study the history of Christ Jesus, we will find that He was one of the most misunderstood human beings in the history of mankind, from His birth to his death. For all you good Christians, who want to know a detailed account of who Jesus was, I highly recommend you read, *"What Did Jesus Really Say?* by Misha'al ibn Abdulla Al-Kadhi.

Our children will not read this history and we as parents will not embrace this body of information and share it with them, because it's too painful to face; or we, simply, don't care. In addition, we have turned on each other in the same way. We have been taught to hate ourselves. We're being destroyed and continue to be subdued, mortified, tortured, killed, and persecuted. That's the real crucifixion.

The Father, the Son and the Holy Spirit

"O People of the Book! Commit no excesses in your religion: nor say of G_d aught but the truth. Christ Jesus, the son of Mary, was (no more than) a Messenger of G_d, and His Word, which He bestowed on Mary, and a Spirit proceeding from Him: So, believe in G_d and His Messengers. Say not, "Trinity": desist: It will be better for you: For G_d is One G_d: Glory be to Him: (Far Exalted is He) above having a son. To Him Belong all things in the heavens and on earth. And enough Is G_d as a Disposer of affairs." (Holy Qur'an 4:171)

As I ponder over this concept, or idea-and this is a concept, or an idea; a bad one at that-this is no more than a shell game. It's like I'm looking for the truth underneath. The Father is, actually, G_d. The Holy Spirit is the Angel/Gabriel and Christ Jesus is the Messenger, who G_d blessed with revelation. Since the beginning of humanity, whoever G_d decides to enlighten, this has always been the aforementioned order, or process given. Many religions possess trinities, or triads; for example, Christianity's Father, Son, and Holy Spirit; Judaic Cabalism's Kether, Cochma, and Binah; ancient Egypt's Osiris, Isis, and Horus; and Hinduism's Brahma, Vishnu, and Shiva. There's nothing new under the sun. As I mentioned in the previous paragraphs above, G_d is not the father of humanity.

Adam is our human father. Christ Jesus was of virgin birth and He had no father, like Adam, who didn't have a father, or a mother. G_d is showing you, through Adam, that He doesn't need the assistant of a woman, nor a man, to create. G_d created the heavens and earth from, literally, nothing. Why would He need children? If you believe in this idea, then you must ask yourself this very important question. Did G_d command us to believe in this concept, or was it the Church? Last, but not least, the Holy Spirit(s), the Angels, Jibril/Gabriel and Michael, have always been the angels of revelation. There is no issue in any theology more obscure and confusing than the beliefs in the trinity and the "sonship" of Jesus Christ. Read the Scripture.

Blind Leading the Blind

You know, everywhere we turn there is confusion, drama and disappointments in our lives. This world didn't give us guidance, or knowledge. It gave us emotions, whether it is in music, movies, social media, or our own personal life. We will never have peace if we continue to hanker after and worship the materials things of this world. If we desire the allurements, or the pomp and glitter, which is what most people want, that's exactly what we will have; a life without light, or guidance; just bling that can blind us to the truth.

Belief in the One G_d will change the whole trajectory of your life. Holding on to monstrous ideas about G_d, calling Him, "the Man upstairs", or saying, He has a mother, referring to Him as "father", or "Heavenly Father", is very disrespectful to G_d. We should not give G_d nicknames. He's the Creator of all systems of knowledge, Lord of all Worlds. You've got Him taking a backseat to Jesus when G_d created Jesus. Some people don't think that G_d hears their prayers, sometimes. If someone called you, John or Mary, and your name is Bob, or Linda, would you answer? The above names you've given Him are names in creation. G_d is our Creator, which means He creates what He wills. He's the Sovereign, the Holy One, the Source of Peace and Perfection, the Guardian of Faith, the Preserver of Safety, the Exalted in Might, the Irresistible, the Supreme. Glory to G_d. (High is He) Above the partners they attribute to Him (Holy Qur'an 59:23). He's the Merciful Benefactor, the Gracious, the Evolver and Redeemer. These are some of G_d's attributes and they are, literally, unlimited. But you only say He's Good. How can you describe G_d like this, using one of the most mediocre words in the English dictionary, saying He created the world in six days and on the seventh day He rested (Sunday)? Now, why would G_d need rest? Many of you go to your houses of worship when you know Sunday is actually the first day of the week.

Saying things about Him you know not will never earn you a life of peace. The uninformed masses want to believe this lie because they don't want to admit they have been wrong, or mislead all this time, while slipping further and further into darkness. If you don't believe this, then just look around you. Look at your friends, people close to you, family members and people in general. They all have one thing in common. Many of them have recurrent problems in their lives. There are people we hear and know about who amass more money and wealth than they need and they're not happy. They're suffering from worry, depression, alcohol addiction, taking all sorts of medication for pain, mental disorder, and even committing suicide.

If your worship was correct do you think you would have all of these ills? Worship the One who created you, not the one the world told you to worship. Our Lord gave Himself to us when He created us. He's in us as He is in all of His creation. G_d's Unity is shown in His creation; yet man will turn to false gods and dispute about the natural way for the human being.

Let Us See G_d

Since the beginning of time, there has always been an inclination for the human family to see G_d. Now, let's examine this phenomenon. In Chapter 7, verse 143 of the Holy Qur'an, Moses said, *"O my Lord! Show Thyself to me that I may look upon Thee"*. *G_d said: "By no means can thou see Me (direct); But look upon the mount; If it abides in its place, then shalt thou see Me"*. *When his Lord manifested His Glory on the Mount, He made it as dust, and Moses fell down in a swoon. When he recovered his senses, he said: "Glory be to Thee! I turn in repentance, and I Am the first to believe"*. In the Bible, in John 1:18 it says: *"No man hath seen G_d at any time."* Exodus 33:20 says, *"And he said, Thou canst not see My Face; for there shall no man see Me and live."* And 1 Timothy 6:16 says, *"Whom no man hath seen nor can see."* These verses confirm that G_d cannot be seen, directly.

This is a test for us, as believers, to believe in the Unseen. To believe in a human, or something physical that the world told us we can see is not a test of our belief, or faith. In religious theology, it says G_d's creation can't take His Glory. The whole world will burn because G_d is of the Unseen, which stands to reason why He couldn't possibly appoint a puny human being as a savior, to save the human family from its sins. Why can't G_d be our savior? Since He's our Creator, this material world we live in has been contaminated with sin, along with our souls. When we pass through this life into the next, our souls have to be cleansed of impurities, if we want to be accepted into the Paradise; otherwise, we can't live in the eternal afterlife. No human being can do this for us. There are no imperfections there. That's the pristine world we're all trying to elevate our lives to. The most ignorant thing humanity can utter is, "Let us see G_d". Now, how can we ask for such a ridiculous request when we can't stand to look at ourselves, with all of our flaws and vices? G_d is Perfect. Our faith should be like Abraham, Moses, Jesus, Muhammed, and all the believers who believed in the Merciful Redeemer.

Removed from The Garden

We have no one to blame for our condition but ourselves. Being driven by hate, jealousy and greed, we have fallen from G_d's Grace. Collectively, we have fashioned this world into unending decadence and debauchery. In every arena we venture into, whether it's politics, religion, entertainment, business or education, we find corruption, because most of us want more than what we really need. When we see someone with more material wealth than what we have, we become jealous. Instead, be happy and inspired by what your brother, or sister have and G_d will bless you to have these things and more. This is the spirit we must adopt and strive for, in the name of G_d and He will bless us, abundantly. If G_d blesses us with material wealth, we can't lose. But if this material wealth is given to us by other than G_d, then it can easily be taken away.

Derogating of His Throne

"Behold! G_d will say: "O Jesus, the son of Mary! Did you say unto men, 'Worship me and my mother as gods in derogation of G_d'?" Jesus will say: "Glory to Thee! Never could I say what I had no right to say. Had I said such a thing, Thou would indeed have known it". (Holy Qur'an 5:116)

Have you ever wondered why, out of all the religions in the world, Christianity is the only one that depicts African Americans making a mockery of their faith? Whenever something good happens to us, we look to the sky and praise Jesus as our lord. How do you know he's up there? Is that supposed to be Heaven/Paradise, or where G_d resides? When we take this position on the location of G_d, or Heaven's whereabouts, we restrict Him and Paradise to a certain locale. G_d is everywhere. He cannot be contained in a specific area, as He is outside of His creation. He is, also, beyond our comprehension.

You sing about Jesus all day, in church. You call him, Lord and Mary, the Mother of G_d. You use G_d and Jesus interchangeably. You play with Him in all your comedy shows and in prayer. You speak of Him in some of your vain expressions. You even made Him a curse word, i.e., "G_d damn!". You have no boundaries when it comes to what you say about G_d, which is very disrespectful. We have gotten so lazy in our worship. We see our friends and relatives on their way to their houses of worship and we ask them to pray for us, when we know we're not living clean.

How lazy is that? Why would you trust someone else with something so sacred as your own salvation? In spite of all this, your, Lord is Oft-Forgiving, Most Merciful. *"Woe to those who join gods with G_d"* (Holy Qur'an 41:6). You have all these different Bibles in circulation, none of which are the same. You have the Masonic Bible, The New International Version Bible, the Mormon Bible, the King James Version 19th Century Bible, the Catholic Bible and so on. Every faith has their own version of the Bible and Sunday, between the hours of 10:00 a.m. to 2:00 p.m., are the most segregated times in America.

Everyone is worshiping in their own way in their different houses of worship. Did you know the Bible was written and designed in a way for the general masses not to understand? How many people do you know who have read the Bible in its entirety? That's because they can't follow it. The meaning of the Bible is in a vault. If you want the keys of understanding to unlock the knowledge of the Bible, read and study the revelation that came afterwards, the Holy Qur'an. You would think, after all this time, someone would have come up with the idea to rewrite the Bible in layman's terms, in order for the masses as a whole to comprehend the message and make their lives better. Throughout the ages, the Bible has undergone many modifications and revisions. Many religious scholars all over the world have proven and testified to this fact.

Michael H. Hart, author of, *The 100: A Ranking of the most Influential Persons in History,* says, "St. Paul, a man who never met Jesus, personally, is the author of the majority of the books of the New Testament, seriously corrupted the teachings of Jesus and substituted them with his own 'version' of Christianity, totally in opposition to that which Jesus and his apostles had taught their followers". Until this day, changes have continued to be made to the Bible for various reasons, primarily, to keep up with the times, political reasons, and to oppress the ignorant masses. But it is not limited to that. Clearly, the Bible has been tampered with by the hands of man. Do you think your Lord would send you revelation that you would not be able to understand? What would be the point? If the Bible was the word of G_d, instead of St. Paul, would all these changes be necessary? No, because G_d would get it right the first time.

We're supposed to be a people of one G_d, but we worship multiple gods in many different ways. This will never bridge the gap of bigotry, prejudice, racism and intolerance between us as long as we continue to worship in this manner. G_d's Word is unchanging. He's the only Truth. It was man who came up with these different "isms" to keep the masses apart, because man knew the only way to do this is by keeping the populace ignorant as to who their Creator truly is.

Our Own Holocaust

This subject is about the death of a people who died to the knowledge of self on every level, over four hundred years ago. By that I mean, they were stripped of their language, identity, culture, and "G_d", when they were stolen from the continent of Africa and transported, like freight, to a foreign land, called America. Thousands upon thousands of Africans were lost in the middle passage; either through death, suicide, murder by the slave master, or through various health reasons. In the history of the human family, no other people on record have ever experienced something so repulsive as the slavery that the African American people experienced in this country, beginning when the first slave ship landed in Jamestown, Virginia in 1619. Some historians say it was in 1555.

There was a time, in the history of this country, when it was against the law for a slave to learn to read; because he/she had to be molded into a tool, or an object, in order to better serve the slave master. There was work to be done and the slave had to be trained to do it. Whatever the job, the slave had to perform the task, whether it was in the house, or the field. If the slave was rebellious, he/she was severely punished by such methods as whipping in front of his/her family members and other slaves; by the slave master and, sometimes, by other co-slave masters. It was a normal occurrence for the slave woman to be raped by the salve master. This is the reason why many of us have different complexions. Our original names were stolen from us and we adopted the slave master's names, i.e., Johnson, or Richardson, etc., upon gaining our freedom; mainly, because these were the only names we knew.

Part of a "rebellious" slave's body might be dismembered by amputating the feet, or cropping his ears. Sometimes, the slave master would blindfold the slave and put him into a room with his mother and make him have sex with her without his knowledge. This is where the term, "motherfucker", was originated. We were taught to hate our black skin, nappy hair, broad noses and each other. For more information on the cruel treatment of our forefathers and mothers, do a google search on the internet for,

58

"Buck breaking". This went on until slavery was finally abolished in 1865.

At this time, the slave was emancipated with no vocation, except for what he/she learned on the plantation; and no education. He/she was faced with many obstacles. Starting from ground zero, the former slave knew that their lives would be filled with many challenges. This was a very tumultuous time for the ex-slave. Although slavery was over, the African American continued to be mistreated through lynching, murder, intimidation, and other atrocities because of his hue and because the laws at that time were against minorities, especially African Americans. Through protest, marches, the Civil Rights Movement, etc., new and improved laws came about. These circumstances created positive change for the freemen, male and female.

Better education for African Americans made possible better jobs, better living conditions and better life in general. If we want to be considered equal along with the rest of humanity, we, as a people, owe it to our fore parents to continue on the journey they started; and continue to make giant steps for our children, their children to come and be the people G_d intended for us to be. There's no excuse why we're in the condition we're in, today. G_d gave our soul the power of choice and a sense of right and wrong. We must do right by ourselves if we want success in our lives. If our people can survive the horrendous treatment in this country, during a time when we were seen as tools, 3/5 human and animals, surely, we can make it now. Most of what we're going though is due to our own self-inflictions. A heavy price was paid by our people before we were ever thought of. If we can't see that, it's our own fault. We stand on the shoulders of the giants in our history, and their accomplishments and yet, we continue to sit around crying and complaining about our individual plights. The same spirit the slaves had in them is no different from the same spirit in us now; after all, they were our parents.

A House Divided

"Behold! Verily to G_d Belong all creatures, in the heavens and on earth. What do they follow who worship as His "partners" other than G_d? They follow nothing but fancy, and they do nothing but lie". (Holy Qur'an 10:66) G_d is One and His Creation is one. This means we (all human beings) were all created from one human soul. Over time, we migrated to different climates of the world and this is how we developed our complexion, speech, features, culture, and our religion, etc. So, no matter what we think, we are a family of one. Since the dawn of the human creation, mankind has been moving towards the division of the human race through the denial and refusal to believe that G_d has no associates. And they, falsely, having no knowledge, attribute to Him sons and daughters. *"Praise and glory be to Him! (far He is) above what they attribute to Him!"* (Holy Qur'an 6:100) This was done to keep the populace ignorant, unyoked, downtrodden, and lost in the wilderness, with no realization of our Creator and who we are as a human race.

This evidence is testimonial to the predicament of the masses all over the world. Being disconnected from the One who created us is the highest form of oppression. We have been separated into many different races, with multiple gods and multiple denominations in numerous houses of worship. We don't have a real connection, or a commonality with each other, because of our diverse concepts of G_d.

Many of us think how we worship makes us better than others. So, we rule over the so-called less fortunate ones with power we think we have. We hide behind our religion as a cloak for wrongdoing. This is one of the reasons for bigotry, prejudice, racism, classicism, imperialism, communism, and capitalism. As long as we follow the wayward direction of this world, we will always be subjected to one of these vices. The earth is our home. G_d created us to live and get along with one another. But we can't seem to do that, because we've been too far removed from our Maker.

Believing our way is better than what G_d said through all of His Messengers and Prophets since our advent on this earth has been our downfall. We think whoever is placed in the White House, our level of education, consulting with psychics, singing and clapping of hands, and trying to be good in our houses of worship on Sunday (and bad as hell through the week) is our salvation. This way of life will never give us a better condition, as long as we continue to distance ourselves from the One who knows and is well-acquainted with all things.

This country has produced some of the greatest minds in the history of the world. It has also spawned some of the most ignorant people where knowledge of G_d is concerned. The truth of the matter is, religion has been shrouded in so much mysticism until the masses don't know what to believe; so, it stands to reason why some people have chosen atheism. We, as human beings, can't stand to be lied to by each other, but we can accept being lied to about who our Creator is. *"Die not, except in the state of submission to the Oft-Forgiving, Most Merciful"*. (Holy Qur'an 2:132) How can we, as a human family, expect to earn the favor of G_d, if we're worshipping the way we want and when we want to? Like it or not, our Merciful Creator gave us a criterion on how He wants us to worship Him. If we, as a family, don't amalgamate ourselves under the worship of the One Creator, this world will always be, "A House Divided!"

Summary

If your worship is wrong, your behavior will follow. Brothers and sisters, if we want a life of peace and tranquility, we must get our own house (worship) in order. If each and every one of us realign and get our lives back in focus, what a glaring difference it would make. Remake our internal world the way G_d intended and, *"He will send you the skies pouring abundant rain, and add strength to your strength"*. (Holy Qur'an 11:52); not the way you want it to be. You see where that got you. There's an author and motivational speaker by the name of, Jim Rohn, who said: "We should work harder on ourselves than on each other".

We must stop taking inventory of and bringing up each other's blemishes, and putting each other down. Concentrate on your own issues. G_d did not put us here to pass judgment on each other. He wants us to love, get along with, and help our brother and sister. If we can accomplish this, and all the things I have said in this small publication, then and only then, can experience paradise and see G_d. By seeing G_d, I don't mean seeing Him with our two eyes. I mean allowing Him to take over and guide our lives. It is worth noting that we have been influenced by this world with chains and shackles of false beliefs, customs, and evil practices. This is a metaphor for human beings' self-imposed abandonment to false values and evil ways that results in the enslavement of the human spirit.

"G_d will never change the Grace which He hath bestowed on a people, until they change what is in their (own) souls. And verily

G_d is He Who heareth and knoweth (all things)." (Holy Qur'an 8:53)

I had a wonderful time bringing this information to the reader. As I said, previously, I hope this book brings benefits and inspires you to greater heights in your lives. I pray that G_d and you, the reader, forgives me for any errors, or misinformation."

"Our Lord! Give us good in this world and good in the Hereafter, and save us from the torment of the Fire." (Holy Qur'an 2:201) *"Behold, Luqman said to his son by way of instruction: 'O my son! Join not in worship (others) with G_d; for false worship is indeed the highest form of oppression'."* (Holy Qur'an 31:13). G_d is One!

The following are excerpts from the Bible and the Holy Qur'an, referencing G_d, the Creator of all Worlds, commanding us, as His human family, on how to worship Him:

Old Testament

"Hear, O Israel: The Lord our G_d is one Lord." (Deuteronomy 6:4)

"Thou shalt have no other gods before Me." (Deuteronomy 5:7)
"Thus saith the Lord the king of Israel and His redeemer the Lord of hosts: I am the first and I am the last; and besides Me there is no G_d." (Isaiah 44:6)

New Testament

"...there is none other G_d but one..." (1 Corinthians 8:4)

64

"...for it is written, you shall worship the Lord your G_d and Him only shall you serve." (Matthew 4:10)

Holy Qur'an

"O People of the Scripture! Do not exceed the limits in your religion, nor say of G_d aught but the truth. The Jesus Christ, the son of Mary was (no more than) an Apostle of G_d and His Word, which He bestowed on Mary, and a spirit proceeding from Him; so, believe in G_d and His Apostles. Say not "(trinity): Desist! It be will better for you; for G_d is one G_d. Glory is to Him (far Exalted is He) above having a son. To Him belongs all things in the heavens and on earth. And enough is God as Disposer of affairs." (Holy Qur'an 4:171)

"So, whoever hopes for the Meeting with his Lord, let him work righteousness and associate none as a partner in the worship of his Lord." (Holy Qur'an 18:110)

Selected Commentaries on Surahs (Chapters) from *"The Holy Qur'an"* - Translation by Abdullah Yusuf Ali

C. 60 - (3:181-200). Regard, unmoved, the taunts of those who laugh at faith; nor let their falsehood nor their seeming prosperity, raise questions in your minds. All who can read the signs of G_d in nature know His wisdom, goodness, power, and justice. They know His promise is sure, and in humble prayer, wholly put their trust in Him.

C. 63 - (4:43-70). Be clean and pure, and seek not occasions for quibbles, nor go after sorcery or false gods. Be faithful in your trusts, learn obedience, and settle your quarrels under the guidance of G_d's Apostle. Ever keep away from hypocrisy and every kind of falsehood. Then will you be admitted to a glorious fellowship with the highest and noblest in the spiritual world.

C. 67 - (4:127-152). Justice to women and orphans is part of religion and the fear of G_d. Stand out firm for justice to all, even against yourselves or your nearest of kin. Remain firm in faith, and consort not with evil or hypocrisy. Be true in speech, and wound not others nor distinguish between teachers of truth, for G_d's Truth is one and should be believed.

C. 69 - (5:1-6). All obligations are sacred, human or divine. In the spiritual world we owe duties to G_d, which must be fulfilled. But whilst we are in this world or sense, those duties are by no means isolated from what we owe to ourselves and our fellows in the world of men. We must respect the laws and customs of the Sacred Mosque and the Sacred Sanctuary. In food our laws are simple: All things good and pure are lawful. We refuse not social intercourse with men and women - People of the Book.

C.74 - (5:87-108). In the physical pleasures of life, the crime is excess: there is no merit in abstention from things that are good and lawful. Take no rash vows, but to solemn oaths be faithful. Shun as abominations drinking and gambling, and superstitions of all kinds. But be reverent to what is sacred in rites and associations. Not the same are things good and things evil. Learn to distinguish, but pry not into questions beyond your ken. Guard your own souls in truth and justice, and no harm can befall you.

C.78 - (6:61-82). G_d's loving care doth encompass us round

throughout life, and delivers us from dangers by land and sea. He is the only protector. How can we then forget Him or run after things that are mere creatures of His, and shall perish - while He is the Eternal G_d, adored by Abraham and all the Prophets?

C.80 - (6:111-129). Those in obstinate rebellion against G_d are merely deceived and deceive each other. Leave them alone, but trust and obey G_d openly and in the inmost recesses of your heart. The plots of the wicked are but plots against their own souls.

C.81 - (6:130-150). G_d punishes not mere shortcoming: There are degrees in good and evil deeds. G_d is Merciful, but His Plan is sure, and none can stand in His way. We must avoid all superstition, and all excess, and humbly ask for His guidance.

C.82 - (6:151-165). G_d's commands are not irrational taboos, but based on the moral law, and conformable to reason. His Way is the straight way, of justice and truth. In unity and faith must we dedicate all our life to His service, and His Alone, to whom we shall return.

C.88 - (7:172-206). Mankind have the nature of good created within them: Yet doth G_d by His Signs keep up a constant reminder to men of His Holy Names. Those who err scarce realize how gradually they fall into sin. Their respite has a term; the doom must come, and it may be on a sudden. So humbly draw nigh to the Lord. Declare His glory, and rejoice in His service.

C.90 - (8:20-37). Be ready to obey G_d's call, and to hold all else as naught: He will give you the light, turn away all evil from you, and forgive you your sins and shortcomings. Ever keep in remembrance His mercies and grace. The godless may try to keep men from G_d, but they will not thrive: They will be hurled together to destruction.

C.94 - (9:30-42). The enemies of faith would fain put out G_d's Light, but G_d's Light will shine more glorious than ever. Wealth is for use and on trust for mankind: hoard not, nor misuse it. Fight a straight fight in the cause of right: go forth bravely to strive and struggle, and prove yourselves worthy of G_d.

C.96 - (9:73-99). The hardest striving and fighting are needed to combat evil and hypocrisy; for sin can reach a stage when the doors of forgiveness are closed. The good must shun all evil as unclean, and gladly welcome all chance of service and sacrifice, as bringing them closer to the Presence and Mercy of G_d.

C.97 - (9:100-118). The vanguard of faith thinks nothing of self-sacrifice. Their reward is G_d's Good Pleasure. Even those who do

wrong but repent will obtain His Mercy; not so Those who persist in unfaith, hypocrisy, and mischief. G_d's Grace is free and abounding for the righteous. Even if they waver or fail, He will turn to them in Mercy, if only they repent and come back unto Him.

C.98 - (9:119-129). To be true in word and deed is to hold our selfish desires at bay, and follow G_d's Call: In this is our fullest satisfaction and reward. But our striving should include study and teaching, for the brother's benefit, for G_d's Message increases our faith and leads us to love Him and trust Him, the Lord of the Throne of Glory Supreme.

C.104 - (11:1-24). G_d's Revelation teaches the Truth: It warns against wrong and gives glad tidings to the righteous: Ungrateful man folds up his heart and fails to see how all Nature points to G_d and to the Hereafter: he but seeks petty issues, forgetting the cause of causes. Not all the wisdom of man can produce aught like the message which comes from G_d, as the Light that leads and the Mercy that forgives. Who then will humble himself before G_d, seeking His Light and His Voice?

C.114 - (13:1-18). G_d's Truth comes to man in revelation and in nature. How noble are His works! How sublime His government of the world! They all declare forth His Glory! Yet man must strangely resist faith, and ask to see the signs of His Power rather than the signs of His Mercy! Doth not His knowledge search through the most hidden things? Are not lightning and thunder the signs of his Might as well as of His Mercy? He alone is worthy of praise, and His Truth will stand when all vanities pass away like scum on the torrent of time.

C.115 - (13:19-31). The seeing and the blind are not alike: Nor are those blessed with faith and those without. The former seek G_d, and attain peace and blessedness in their hearts, and a final home of rest: The latter are in a state of curse, and their end is terrible. If G_d, in His wisdom, postpones retribution, it is for a time. His Promise never fails: it will come to pass in His own good time. In all things it is for Him to command.

C.117 - (14:1-27). Revelation leads mankind from the depths of darkness into light. It comes to every age and nation in its own language. So was it before; so, it is always. The Prophets were doubted, insulted, threatened, and persecuted, but their trust was sure in G_d. It is evil that will be wiped out. G_d's Truth is a goodly tree, firmly established on its roots, stretching its branches high and wide, and bearing good fruit at all times.

C.119 - (15:1-25). G_d's Truth makes all things clear, and He will guard it. But His Signs are not for those who mock. Who fails to see the majesty, beauty, order, and harmony blazoned in His Creation, and His Goodness to all His creatures, in the heavens and on earth? With Him are the sources of all things, and He doth freely give His Gifts in due measure. He holds the keys of life and death, and He will remain when all else passes away.

C.120 - (15:26-50). Man's origin was from dust, lowly; but his rank was raised above that of other creatures because G_d breathed into him His Spirit. Jealously and arrogance caused the fall of Satan, the power of evil: But no power has evil over those sincere souls who worship G_d and seek His Way. Many are the gates of evil, but peace and dignified joy will be the goal of those whom the Grace of G_d has made His Own.

C.123 - (16:1-25). G_d's Command must inevitable come to pass. But all His Creation proclaims His glory, and leads to His Truth. In all things has He furnished man with favors innumerable, to lead and guide him and bring him to Himself. Why then does man refuse the truth, except for arrogance? Why does he run after false gods, thus acting against his own light and misleading other less blest in knowledge?

C.124 - (16:26-50). In all ages wicked men tried to plot against G_d's Way, but they never succeeded, and were covered with shame in ways unexpected. The righteous see good in G_d's Word, and their goal is the good. Great teachers were sent to all nations, to warn against evil and guide to the right. The penalty for evil comes in many unexpected ways, for evil is against nature. And all nature proclaims G_d's Glory and humbly serves Him, the Lord Supreme.

C. 125 - (16:51-83). There is but One G_d, He Who gives all blessings to man and other creatures. His greatest Gift is that He reveals Himself. But in many tangible ways He cares for man and provides for his growth and sustenance. In rain, in milk, in fruits and honey, and in nature and the life of man, with his opportunities of social, moral, and spiritual growth, are signs for those who understand. Why then does man show ingratitude by going after false gods and forgetting G_d?

C. 127 - (16:101-128). G_d's Truth may come in stages, but it gives strength, guidance, and glad tidings, and should be held fast when once received. Be not like those who get puffed up with pride in worldly good, and scorn the truth. Enjoy the good things of life, but render thanks to G_d and obey His Law. Be true in faith, and proclaim His Word with gentle, patient wisdom: for G_d is with those who live in self-restraint a pure, good, and righteous life.

C. 128 - (17:1-22). It is the privilege of the men of G_d to see the most sublime mysteries of the spiritual world and instruct men in righteousness; they warn and shield men against evil. But nothing can lessen each soul's personal responsibility for its own deeds. It carries its faith round its own neck. G_d's Gifts are for all, but not all receive the same gifts, nor are all gifts of equal dignity or excellence.

C.130 - (17:41-60). There is none like unto G_d. Exalted beyond measure is He. Creation declares His Glory. His revelation is truth, but is beyond comprehension to those who believe not in the hereafter. Those who serve Him should beware lest words unseemly should escape them, whether to friend or foe. Avoid dissensions, and know that G_d's Wrath when kindled is a terrible thing. But we rejoice that He forbears and forgives.

C.134 - (18:23-44). True knowledge is with G_d alone. We are not to dispute on matters of conjecture, but to rely on the truth that comes from G_d. As in the parable, the man who piles up wealth and is puffed up with this world's goods, despising those otherwise endowed, will come to an evil end, for his hopes were not built on G_d.

C.135 - (18:45-59). The life of this world is ephemeral, and its gains will not last. Good deeds are the best of possessions in G_d's sight: All will be levelled up on the Day of Judgement, and a new order created on the basis of truth, according to the Book of Deeds. Pride is the root of evil, rebellion, and wrong. Who will choose evil ones in preference to G_d? Let us accept truth, for though falsehood may flourish for a time, it must perish in the end.

C.142 - (20:1-8). G_d's revelation is not an occasion for man's distress: it is a message to show that G_d the All-Knowing sits on the throne of Mercy and guides all affairs. There is no G_d but He; to Him belong all the most beautiful names.

C. 48 - (21:30-50). Look at G_d's creation: contemplate its unity of design and benevolence of purpose. Death must come to all, but life and faith are not objects of ridicule. Truth will outlast all mockery: 'tis G_d Who calls, because He cares for you, and on His Judgment Seat will weigh each act, each thought, each motive, great or small, with perfect justice. Come, Ye all, reject not His Blessed Message.

C. 150 - (21:94-112). No good deed is fruitless: work while yet there's time: for with judgement the door will be closed to repentance. No false gods of fancy can help. The righteous will have no fear; for them the angelic greetings will truly open a new world, which they will inherit. This was G_d's Message of old, and the same is G_d's Message renewed: for G_d is one, and so is His Message, proclaimed for all, freely and in loving truth.

C. 172 - (27:59-93). G_d's Goodness and Mercy are manifest through all nature and in the heart and conscience of man. He alone knows all: our knowledge can at best be partial. Yet we can travel through space and time and see how evil never prospered. G_d teaches us good, but how can we see if we make ourselves blind? At the end of all things shall we know how small is our state, but for G_d's Grace: let us bow to His Will and accept His true Guidance: Let us praise Him and trust Him-now and forever!

"O You, the only One we worship! We cannot attain to true knowledge of You, yet we believe that You are nearer to us than our jugular veins. We feel Your existence and nearness in the depths of our hearts through the universe, which You created and opened to us like a book, and through the wonderful harmony of form between all parts of Your creation. We come to perceive that we are integrated into the whole realm of Your theophanies, and thus our souls are rested and consoled, and our hearts find serenity. (Excerpted from, *Question & Answers about Islam Vol. 1,* by M. Fethulla Gulen).

ABOUT THE AUTHOR

Tyrell Nasheed Thabit is a deeply spiritual man who has spent over 30 years studying religion, African American literature and various other subjects. He brings a wealth of knowledge to his book, "Earnest Seekers of Truth". He has taken various passages and information from Scripture and African American literature and brought them to the forefront as they relate to issues we face every day. Mr. Thabit has always had a burning passion for knowledge. He's a 10-year U.S. Navy Veteran, who served in both Persian Gulf Wars; the first war during his tenure in the U. S. Navy, and the second while serving in the U. S. Merchant Marines.

He's currently a merchant mariner, who has spent the last 30 years traveling the world. He, also, did an around the world tour in 2013. He has been married for 24 years and has two children. His inspiration to write this book was because of his own personal struggle with poor choices and a deep desire to be a better human being and a G_d-fearing person. It is his hope that the reader will receive the same enjoyment in reading, "Earnest Seekers of Truth," as the author received in writing this book.

It is Mr. Thabit's intent that this book will inspire you, the reader, to elevate your life in a very positive and spiritual way.

Enjoy!